Big Bears at Brooks Falls

Photos by Mark Kostich

Written by Jessica Lee Anderson

Paperback ISBN: 978-1-964078-36-6

To everyone who works to conserve bears and wildlife, and to Mark Kostich, thanks for making this book a possibility given your talents and amazing adventures! - JLA

Bears identifications and date, if known: Front cover: Bear 128 Grazer and yearling (2021); Interior cover page: Bear 128 Grazer and cubs (2021); Dedication page: Bear 402's cubs (2018); P. 8 Bear 402 (2018), P. 9: Bear 32 Chunk (2020); P. 10: Bear 909 or 910; P. 15: 854 Divot and cubs; P: 16: Bear 747; P. 17: Bear 821 Pepper (2023); P. 18: Bear 151 Walker; P. 19: Unknown bear eating a pink salmon (humpy); P. 22: Bear 909 (left) and Bear 128 Grazer (right); P. 23: Bear 94's cubs (2022); P. 25: Bear 480 Otis (2013); P. 26: Bear 409 Beadnose; P. 27: Bear 128 Grazer and cubs (2021); P: 28: 854 Divot and cubs; Backmatter: Bear 42 and cubs (2021); Back cover: Bear 171 (2021)

All photos taken by Mark Kostich apart from P. 4: Bamse031P (den), P.32: Michael Anderson

This Book Belongs to:

_____

What do the brown bears at Katmai National Park and Preserve dream of as they slumber away winter to avoid starvation? In their earthen dens they dug with claws longer than some human fingers, the snow keeping them insulated and cozy, do they twitch in their sleep, imagining berry bushes and an abundance of salmon at Brooks Falls? What are their first thoughts when they stir as snow retreats in spring, apart from extreme hunger?

And what about the hundreds of thousands of salmon migrating, do they daydream as they travel from the ocean, preparing to surge upriver? Do they recall smells and tastes where they hatched years ago, where they hope to return to spawn? Or are they so driven by instinct that they focus every effort on moving forward despite the risks, even encountering a waterfall they must leap over? Are they aware of how much they'll change by the end of their journey or how important they are to Katmai's ecosystems?

Like beloved Bear 402 did for many seasons with eight known litters, mother bears emerge from the den with cubs to safeguard and teach. Some cubs will have been born that very winter, cubs-of-the-year, also known as COY, while other cubs will be yearlings, a year or two old. They'll stay by their mother's side for as long as possible, learning to be bears and clinging to her wisdom and protection until it is time to separate.

The world is challenging for brown bears, often marked by losses and wins, especially for cubs. They face frequent threats from animals, including from other bears. Mama bears watch over them the best they can, like guiding them up a tree for safety if a threat looms. As cubs grow, they'll become braver and more adventurous.

No longer babies, but not yet mature adults, subadult bears must learn how to survive on their own and discover their place in the hierarchy, or social ranking, of bears. Perhaps they'll become dominant bears someday, or maybe they'll continue to survive by avoiding risks and the dangers of large adult bears.

Dominant bears are usually confident, massive males (known as boars). Boars sometimes suffer battle scars and broken bones as they fight for courtship rights or over territory. Bear 32, Chunk, would later endure several injuries since this photo was taken. Bear rank changes when dominant bears step back and large, robust bears charge aggressively ahead.

During the main sockeye salmon run, brown bears crowd Brooks Falls. The waterfall creates a natural obstacle that the fish must hurdle, slowing their journey and making them easier to catch. A brown bear's fishing station is determined by bear hierarchy.

Brown bears gobble up as much as they can during late spring, summer, and part of fall to gain weight in preparation for winter hibernation that can last up to six months. While brown bears will eat grass, nuts, fruit, and more, salmon is a good source of protein and fats, helping the bears to quickly pack on the pounds.

While brown bears see and hear similar to humans, their sense of smell is a superpower, much stronger than a dog's sense of smell. Besides displaying dominance, bears stand on their hind legs to get a better view or catch a whiff of something in the air. Smell helps bears find food and serves as another form of communication, beyond grunts, huffs, and growls. Scents inform brown bears about potential mates, dominance, and dangers.

The Jacuzzi, a deep pool at the base of Brooks Falls, is a popular spot where brown bears use their senses to catch fish. Salmon rest in the teaming waters of the Jacuzzi before attempting to leap over the waterfalls. Not all jumps will be successful, though many salmon will make it across.

Some brown bears literally go out on a limb to find food, keeping watch for thieves or competitors ready to run them off. Wary bears may prefer to fish downstream from busy Brooks Falls, like in the Riffles, a shallow zone with water quickly flowing over the rocks. Brown bears are good swimmers and can swim faster than humans. On land, they're speedy sprinters, capable of outrunning even the fastest person.

Female bears, known as sows, sometimes avoid the crowded Falls too, seeking food in quieter locations like Lower Brooks River. There may be less food available here and elsewhere compared to the Falls, but it is a sacrifice a mother bear might make for the safety of her cubs, even if she needs all the energy she can get to produce milk for them. Mother bears teach cubs how to fish and find other food—skills and techniques that stay with them their entire lives.

Other bears prefer to fish in the Far Pool, especially those unsure about human visitors on nearby viewing platforms. While some bears get used to having people around, or habituated, other bears never do and will try to avoid them, even if it means fewer feasts. The Brooks Falls Brown Bear Cam allows an enormous number of viewers to enjoy the bears online without the cost and challenges of travel or any added stress to the bears or environment.

Brown bears are intelligent and will find ways to adapt and overcome challenges. They each have distinct personalities and behaviors, including different methods of fishing, like pouncing, lunging, snorkeling, or diving. Some brown bears will wait to catch a fish mid-jump on the Lip of Brooks Falls.

Brown bears are some of the largest, strongest bears on the planet! They have powerful muscles, and their skeletons are thick enough to support hefty weight. Boars can weigh well over 1,000 pounds (453 kgs)! Katmai's coastal brown bears are the same species as inland brown bears, often referred to as grizzlies. Coastal brown bears grow larger because they have access to more food sources such as salmon.

As fall approaches, bears will increase the amount of time they spend gorging on food and filling out. The fatter, the better as bears will lose up to a quarter to a third of their entire body weight during hibernation. Larger bears can eat well over forty salmon in one day! In seasons of plenty, they may practice high-grading, eating only the nutrient dense parts of salmon—skin, brains, and the eggs called roe.

Salmon leftovers will be devoured by gulls, ravens, bald eagles, wolves, and more, including the lowest ranked bears—cubs. Remains release crucial nutrients into the soil and the water. Salmon are called keystone species because the health of Katmai and surrounding areas depends upon their presence.

Bears aren't apt to share. Arguments occasionally occur over food or access to a favorite fishing location. Bears usually prefer to intimidate rather than physically fight, though quarrels might lead to noisy brawls, bites, powerful swipes, and claw slashes.

A mother bear will often go to battle and fight for her cubs if they get caught in a dangerous situation. Fearless and ready to grapple if needed, Bear 128, Grazer, has been one of the most dominant, top-ranking sows to have frequented Brooks Falls.

Always watching and mimicking, cubs will playfully spar together. Play fighting helps cubs learn how to defend themselves while building strength and coordination.

Bears aren't the only ones battling it out during this time of binging and bulking up. Human Bear Cam viewers from all over the world vote on which brown bear they believe has achieved the most success and rotundness to become Fat Bear Week champion. Pudgy cubs are candidates for Fat Bear Junior.

Bear 480, Otis, was crowned winner of Fat Bear Tuesday when the competition started in 2014. The tournament grew from one day to seven days, now ending on Fat Bear Tuesday. Otis was known for fishing in the Far Pool, a place that became referred to as his "office" because he put in so many hours there. His ability to plump up to massive proportions helped him win again in 2016, 2017, and 2021.

Bear 409, Beadnose, triumphantly tanked up on enough salmon to get into the Fat Bear Week Hall of Fame, winning the title in 2015 and 2018. Brown bears often have quirks and features that set them apart, like Beadnose's nose. Brown bears at Brooks Falls sometimes receive nicknames in addition to the identification number assigned to them by Bear Monitors for tracking and management purposes.

Bear 128, Grazer, won Fat Bear Week in 2023 and 2024. Stout and strong, this popular sow became skilled at catching fish on the prized Lip of Brooks Falls, an area usually occupied by dominant boars. Here she is in this photo teaching techniques to her cubs.

At the end of the season, when food becomes harder to find, the big bears at Brooks Falls slow down as they have done for generations. They'll once again carve earthen dens with claws as long as some human fingers, ready to hunker down for winter.

The Brooks Falls Brown Bear Cam goes offline in late fall when the bears move to dens carved into nearby mountains, lessons of resilience and determination passed on to millions of viewers worldwide. Perhaps admirers are left dreaming of ways to protect these wild bears and their natural spaces.

Katmai National Park and Preserve is remote, and the only way to get there is by plane or boat. This is a photo of photographer Mark Kostich taken on one of his many trips to Alaska.

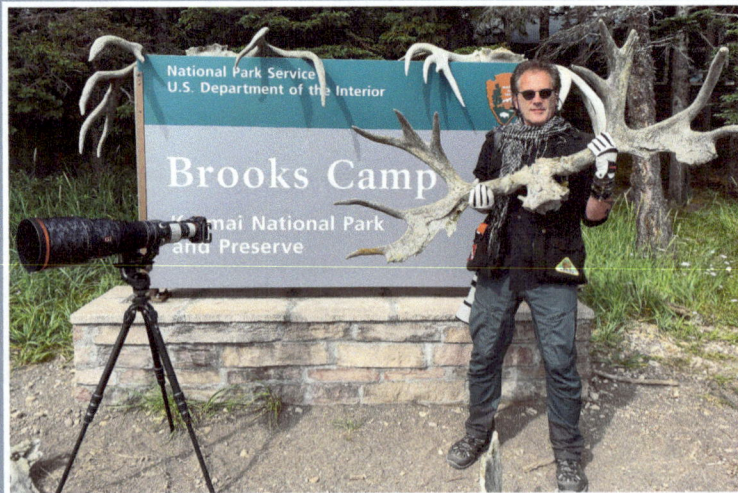

Upon arrival at Brooks Camp, visitors must attend "bear school," a safety orientation program. Visitors learn about giving bears distance (at least fifty feet), and the importance of paying attention and following rules (such as only eating in safe locations). Rules keep both humans and bears safe!

Staying vigilant is important as is listening to Park Rangers and the staff. After visiting Brooks Falls Platform, Mark arrived back at his cabin to find Bear 42 and her cubs chewing on the wood! Park Rangers gently encouraged the bears to move along.

Enjoy breathtaking views and wildlife viewing opportunities at Brooks Falls from summer to late fall by visiting: https://explore.org/livecams/brown-bears. Visit https://katmaiconservancy.org to learn more about Fat Bear Week and ways to help protect Katmai National Park and Preserve.

About the Author and Photographer

Jessica Lee Anderson is an award-winning author of over 100 books for young readers. Jessica loves spending time in nature and exploring the outdoors with her husband, Michael, and their daughter, Ava! She dreams of visiting as many national parks as possible in her lifetime. You can learn more about Jessica by visiting www.jessicaleeanderson.com.

Mark Kostich is an international wildlife photographer who travels the globe. His work can be found in publications by National Geographic, Animal Planet, Discovery Channel, Smithsonian, American Museum of Natural History, and many, many more. His travels have taken him to Laos, Vietnam, Thailand, Kenya, Tanzania, Ecuador, Costa Rica and Guatemala, among many other places. Visit www.bearsofbrooksfalls.com for more information.

www.ingramcontent.com/pod-product-compliance
Lightning Source LLC
Chambersburg PA
CBHW061145030426
42335CB00002B/110